Susan Unterberg

HENRI COLE

BLACKBIRD
AND WOLF

Henri Cole was born in Fukuoka, Japan, and was raised in Virginia. The recipient of many awards, he is the author, most recently, of *Middle Earth*, a Pulitzer Prize finalist, and *The Visible Man*. He lives in Boston.

BLACKBIRD AND WOLF

HENRI COLE

BLACKBIRD
AND WOLF

FARRAR STRAUS GIROUX

NEW YORK

FARRAR, STRAUS AND GIROUX
18 West 18th Street, New York 10011

Printed in the United States of America
Published in 2007 by Farrar, Straus and Giroux
First paperback edition, 2008

The Library of Congress has cataloged the hardcover edition as follows:
Cole, Henri.
    Blackbird and wolf / Henri Cole.— 1st ed.
        p. cm.
    ISBN-13: 978-0-374-11379-7 (hardcover : alk. paper)
    ISBN-10: 0-374-11379-3 (hardcover : alk. paper)
    I. Title.

PS3553.O4725B57 2007
811'.54—dc22

                                      2006026133

Paperback ISBN-13: 978-0-374-53112-6
Paperback ISBN-10: 0-374-53112-9

www.fsgbooks.com

FOR MY BROTHERS

The diver descends naked,

until exhausted, drawing up the sink-stone,

then the oysters, only to plunge again

into the onyx river, which, like love,

cannot grant one everything

while transfiguring the color, form,

and meaning of existence.

CONTENTS

III : DUNE

BIRTHDAY

SYCAMORES

I came from a place with a hole in it,

my body once its body, behind a beard of hair.

And after I emerged, all dripping wet,

heavy drops came out of my eyes, touching its face.

I kissed its mouth; I bit it with my gums.

I lay on it like a snail on a cup,

my body, whatever its nature was,

revealed to me by its body. I did not know

I was powerless before a strange force.

I did not know life cheats us. All I knew,

nestling my head in its soft throat pouch,

was a hard, gemlike feeling burning through me,

like limbs of burning sycamores, touching

across some new barrier of touchability.

Polishing your eyeglasses, I try them on

and watch the nurses hoist you—blind, giggling,

muttering nonsense French. For a moment, like a spider,

you dangle at the edge of the present,

pondering who I am: "Ma, I'm Henri.

You made me." Then my eyes flee the here-and-now.

You're pulling yourself out of the deep end,

your skin like the seamless emulsion on a strip of film.

Sensuality is confirming beauty. I'm eleven again.

Then the banal shatters everything.

In a tangled nightgown, your skin marsupial,

you're pawing through leaf mulch for pain medicine

you can't function without. The thrash of your hands

smolders like wet black ash.

In Chinese, the basic phonetic value of horse, *ma*,

turns up in the word for mother.

"Horse-mother, look!" I cry. Soldier-ants

are suckling on the big pink heads of your peonies.

Horse-mother flickers like a candle in the dark.

Horse-mother, why does your mouth have a grim set?

I know that all beneath the sky decays.

I know that you once cradled me in sleep,

your belly empty as a purse. "Horse-mother, look!"

I repeat. The mimosa tree is going to sleep,

its tiny pinnate leaves closing and drooping,

like you, sensitive to light and touch,

mimicking death when I push a needle into you

and bright beads run out, as from a draining bird.

Naked, hairy, trembling, I dove into the green,

where I saw a bulky form that was Mother

in her pink swimsuit, pushing out of water,

so I kicked deeper, beyond a sugar boat

and Blake's Ulro and Beulah; beyond grief, fate;

fingers, toes, and skin; beyond speech,

plagues of the blood, and flowers thrown on a coffin;

beyond Eros and the disease of incompleteness;

and as I swam I saw myself against the sky

and against the light, a tiny human knot with eyes,

my numb hands and repeated motion, like the gulls aloft,

touching the transparent structure of the world,

and in that icy, green, silvery frothing,

I was straightening all that I had made crooked.

OIL & STEEL

My father lived in a dirty-dish mausoleum,

watching a portable black-and-white television,

reading the Encyclopaedia Britannica,

which he preferred to Modern Fiction.

One by one, his schnauzers died of liver disease,

except the one that guarded his corpse

found holding a tumbler of Bushmills.

"Dead is dead," he would say, an anti-preacher.

I took a plaid shirt from the bedroom closet

and some motor oil—my inheritance.

Once, I saw him weep in a courtroom—

neglected, needing nursing—this man who never showed

me much affection but gave me a knack

for solitude, which has been mostly useful.

Gentleness had come a great distance to be there,

I thought, as paramedics stanched the warm blood,

signaling one another with their eyes.

I was not as I was, and I didn't know why,

so I was aware of a shattering, of an unbidden,

moving under the influence of a restoring force.

Like a Japanese fan folding, my spirit seemed possessed

of such a simple existence, the sexual principle

no longer at its center, nor memory.

I felt like the personification of an abstraction,

like mercy. My hands were red and swollen.

A great chain, the twitch of my life, dragged against decay.

Then I heard shouts. Far off, a horse whinnied.

I blinked back tears as I was lifted forth.

CHENIN BLANC

"Hey, human, my heart feels bad,"

a crow asserts, as I am reading and drinking

chenin blanc on the balcony. His buddy

is sampling a limp rodent and seems

to want to say something, holding out

a clenched yellow foot, like a tiny man:

"Whatever you want, want it for yourself,"

he beaks, quoting Rumi, plainly disappointed,

but also kind of visionary, as if his crow mind

senses my own private Hell. Still, my hands

rubbing my neck have the intensity

of a mother's, touching a child, so I say,

"Talk to me, crow," defending the human,

"Didn't God make flesh feel this?"

I didn't know what to do with myself,

arriving through woods and fields at the lake.

The world of instinct, crying out at night

(its grief so human), frightened me,

so I scribbled vainly, contemplating the surface

of the water, frolicking in it until my long,

amphibious body, covered in fine hairs—

with whiskers, moles, and a blunt nose—

became terra cotta brown, and I—usually nocturnal—

slept all night and ate omnivorously

(eggs, fish, berries, and honey), and, after a few weeks,

the puny ingredients of my life vanished.

I, upright on hind legs, alternatively sexed

(even that seemed banal), didn't want to go home.

TWILIGHT

There's a black bear

in the apple tree

and he won't come down.

I can hear him panting,

like an athlete.

I can smell the stink

of his body.

Come down, black bear.

Can you hear me?

The mind is the most interesting thing to me;

like the sudden death of the sun,

it seems implausible that darkness will swallow it

or that anything is lost forever there,

like a black bear in a fruit tree,

gulping up sour apples

with dry sucking sounds,

or like us at the pier, somber and tired,

making food from sunlight,

you saying a word, me saying a word, trying hard,

though things were disintegrating.

Still, I wanted you,

your lips on my neck,

your postmodern sexuality.

Forlorn and anonymous:

I didn't want to be that. I could hear

the great barking monsters of the lower waters

calling me forward.

You see, my mind takes me far,

but my heart dreams of return.

Black bear,

with pale-pink tongue

at the center of his face,

is turning his head,

like the face of Christ from life.

Shaking the apple boughs,

he is stronger than I am

and seems so free of passion—

no fear, no pain, no tenderness. I want to be that.

Come down, black bear,

I want to learn the faith of the indifferent.

As I light the oven to warm up dinner,

I watch a fly make an exploration

of the room, where I've hung wet clothes.

My human fingers, with their long, slender bones,

appear more like a reptile's. I don't know,

perhaps there's no meaning in all this,

like a slit in the grassy earth, from which rodents

come and go. Mud and life, water and hope—

I want them all, really. Instead, I listen

to a blood-dyed fist *tap-tap* inside my skull

and entertain a miserable fly.

In a short while, he'll run down,

like my wristwatch, but my warm human breath

will make him fly again.

TO SLEEP

Then out of the darkness leapt a bare hand

that stroked my brow, "Come along, child;

stretch out your feet under the blanket.

Darkness will give you back, unremembering.

Do not be afraid." So I put down my book

and pushed like a finger through sheer silk,

the autobiographical part of me, the *am*,

snatched up to a different place, where I was

no longer my body but something more—

the compulsive, disorderly parts of me

in a state of equalization, everything sliding off:

war, suicide, love, poverty—as the rebellious,

mortal I, I, I lay, like a beetle irrigating a rose,

my red thoughts in a red shade all I was.

By now,

I think I have been

entirely erased:

my humorous glances

polished out of the mirror,

my young gray hairs vacuumed from the carpet,

where each night I undressed,

my worries beaten out of the pillows,

my oils daubed from the upholstery.

It's like removing a corpse from a sarcophagus,

I think, an intelligent man

who thinks too much,

speaks little,

and doesn't want to leave love behind.

I care nothing about respectability.

I can bear to think of the brisk and ruthless present

cropped short like a donkey's ears;

I can bear to think of Heaven and Hell,

where there is no tennis or jam;

but I can't bear to think of the trough in my mattress

filled up by another.

So when the erasers arrive,

smiling placidly, spraying everything with chemicals,

"Hey," I shout, touching my chest,

feeling a giant, tangible lust,

"not me!"

Peeling oranges, cracking walnuts at dawn,

I feel like I'm headed toward

some kind of new humanism.

I'm tired of just being a man.

Will I look back on my life as on a delicately reflective painting?

I don't know. My teeth need brushing,

the bed isn't made, I want work,

and Wednesday is flaring up,

like a cut lily no eraser can kill.

THE TREE CUTTERS

You can't see them and then you can,

like bear cubs in the treetops working for man,

hoisting one another with ropes and pulleys

that seem the clearest possible metaphor

for bright feelings vs. dark feelings,

as I lie in the grass below, hearing the big limbs fall,

like lightning exploding on the lake.

Once, a thick, dirty, bad-smelling sorrow

covered me like old meat: I saw a blood-stained toad,

instead of my white kitten; I saw shadows and misprision,

instead of my milk and pancakes. "Maybe God has gone away,"

my life moaned, hugging my knees, my teeth, my terrible pride,

though, after a time, like a warm chrysalis, it produced

a tough, lustrous thread the pale yellow of onions.

When I was a boy, we called it punishment

to be locked up in a room. God's apparent

abdication from the affairs of the world

seemed unforgivable. This morning,

climbing five stories to my apartment,

I remember my father's angry voice

mixed with anxiety and love. As always,

the possibility of home—at best an ideal—

remains illusory, so I read Plato, for whom love

has not been punctured. I sprawl on the carpet,

like a worm composting, understanding things

about which I have no empirical knowledge.

Though the door is locked, I am free.

Like an outdated map, my borders are changing.

SELF-PORTRAIT WITH HORNETS

Hornets, two hornets, buzz over my head;

I'm napping and cannot keep my eyes open.

"Do you come from far away?" I ask, dozing off.

My gums are dry when I wake. A morning breeze

rakes the treetops. I can smell the earth.

The two hornets are puzzling over

something sticky on my night table,

wiping their gold heads with their arms.

Ordinary things are like symbols. My eyes are watery

and blurred. Then I lose myself again.

I'm walking slowly in a heat haze,

my vision contracting to a tiny porthole,

drawing me to it, like flourishing palms.

I can feel blood draining out of my face.

I can feel my heart beating inside my heart,

the self receding from the center of the picture.

I can taste sugar under my tongue.

All the usual human plots of ascent

and triumph appear disrupted.

Crossing my ankles, I watch the day

vibrate around me, watch the geraniums

climb toward the distant mountains

where I was born, watch the black worm

wiggling out of the window box,

hiding its head from the pale sun

that lies down on everything,

purifying it. Lord, teach me to live.

Teach me to love. Lie down on me.

GRAVITY
AND
CENTER

GRAVITY AND CENTER

I'm sorry I cannot say I love you when you say

you love me. The words, like moist fingers,

appear before me full of promise but then run away

to a narrow black room that is always dark,

where they are silent, elegant, like antique gold,

devouring the thing I feel. I want the force

of attraction to crush the force of repulsion

and my inner and outer worlds to pierce

one another, like a horse whipped by a man.

I don't want words to sever me from reality.

I don't want to need them. I want nothing

to reveal feeling but feeling—as in freedom,

or the knowledge of peace in a realm beyond,

or the sound of water poured in a bowl.

I see you sitting erect on my fire escape,

plucking at your dinner of flayed mouse,

like the red strings of a harp, choking a bit

on the venous blue flesh and hemorrhaging tail.

With your perfect black-and-white thief's mask,

you look like a stuffed bird in a glass case,

somewhere between the animal and human life.

The love word is far away. Can you see me?

I am a man. No one has what I have:

my long clean hands, my bored lips. This is my home:

Woof-woof, the dog utters, afraid of emptiness,

as I am, so my soul attaches itself to things,

trying to create something neither confessional

nor abstract, like the moon breaking through the pines.

LOONS

Propped up on your elbow at the foot

of the bed—animal, inward, bare—

you make me want to shield my body.

Between us there is a covenant:

Though I'm stronger than you, I do

what you want. A chemical, stimulating

the thinnest wires of your brain, makes me

as desirable to you as you are to me.

Still, everything feels fractured and bruised.

A globe of fog encompasses the bed,

like night water, on which loons—drifting separately,

mated for life—wail to one other,

their strange, larval nakedness something good,

instead of a kind of helplessness.

This is the time of year the missing ones

come back to us—no longer weighted down

by debris, curled into fetal positions,

rising naked through the murky water—

as if they can hear our yelling shouts

as we dive from the ledges above,

pretending they are not there.

Life piles onto life. "Come," says

the onyx water, "come into my deep,"

and I run across the grass into the fizzy air—

insane, undignified—but even there,

falling through the lavender haze, I extend

my arms to you, my secret comrade,

who made me love you.

HOMOSEXUALITY

First I saw the round bill, like a bud;

then the sooty crested head, with avernal eyes

flickering, distressed, then the peculiar

long neck wrapping and unwrapping itself,

like pity or love, when I removed the stovepipe

cover of the bedroom chimney to free

what was there and a duck crashed into the room

(I am here in this fallen state), hitting her face,

bending her throat back (my love, my inborn

turbid wanting, at large all night), backing away,

gnawing at her own wing linings (the poison of my life,

the beast, the wolf), leaping out the window,

which I held open (now clear, sane, serene),

before climbing back naked into bed with you.

I sit on the dock for a haircut and watch

as summer spreads out, relieving the general,

indiscriminate gray, like a mouthful of gin

spreading out through the capillaries

of my brain, etherizing everything

it is too painful to think or say,

as I dangle my feet in the water,

like bits of a man. On the goldenrod,

Japanese beetles are holding an orgy.

The green snake throws off its enameled skin.

And somewhere—invisible as the avenues

of the dead—a small door is left open for love,

pushing and pulling at each of us, as the water

pushes and pulls at my cut gray hairs.

TOXICOLOGY

Here, all night, in locked Ward C, they arrive,

like moist, limp hands tied fast to nothing.

Asleep or awake, in the somber light

of dream or nocturnal data-processing,

life undeaths itself, as if it really were

a limitless map of transparent blue lines

leading us out of captivity,

out of the masochistic desire

to crush and be crushed in turn,

and out of paranoid dissembling.

Here, in the nightmare border country of overdoses—

where the worm's mouth sucks

and God, our Father, feeds the altar flame

—my task is to give, empathize, and love him.

Waking from comalike sleep, I saw the poppies,

with their limp necks and unregimented beauty.

Pause, I thought, say something true: It was night,

I wanted to kiss your lips, which remained supple,

but all the water in them had been replaced

with embalming compound. So I was angry.

I loved the poppies, with their wide-open faces,

how they carried themselves, beckoning to me

instead of pushing away. The way in and the way out

are the same, essentially: emotions disrupting thought,

proximity to God, the pain of separation.

I loved the poppies, with their effortless existence,

like grief and fate, but tempered and formalized.

Your hair was black and curly; I combed it.

BOWL OF LILACS

My lilacs died today, floating in a bowl.

All week I watched them pushing away,

their pruned heads swollen together into something

like anger, making a brief comeback

toward the end, as if secretly embalmed.

Just before your death, I cut your hair,

so when you were laid out you looked like yourself.

Then some men screwed planks over your coffin.

I held a towel to my face. Once, in a light-bathed kitchen,

naked and blissfully myself, I scrambled us eggs

and felt the act of looking and perceiving

was no longer something understood

from the exterior. It was pure being:

saturated and raw as a bowl of lilacs.

Outstretched in the tub, like a man in a tomb,

I pull the razor across my face and throat.

The bathroom is pristine, spare, without any clear

conflict; I like that. The cells in my skin

draw heat to themselves, like grape bunches.

In the silver hand mirror, my youthful

shyness is gone now. I lie bent, turned in,

but supple, pliant. I was rough on you;

I know this because you told me, but you

held up well. Trees, mammals, fire, snow—

they are like emotions. Through our eyes,

pain comes in (my doctor told me this),

but how does it exit, if you're looking forward

and I'm looking back, my big, unlovely head

(you called it that) feverish, then shivery?

MY WEED

On the path to the water, I found an ugly weed

growing between rocks. The wind was stroking it,

saying, "My weed, my weed." Its solid,

hairy body rose up, with big silver leaves

that rubbed off on me, like sex. At first,

I thought it was a lamb's ear, but it wasn't.

I'm not a member of the ugly school,

but I circled around it and looked a lot,

which is to say, I was just being, and it seemed to me—

in a higher sense—to represent the sanity of living.

It was twilight. Planets were gathering.

"Mr. Weed," I said, "I'm competitive,

I'm afraid, I'm isolated, I'm bright.

Can you tell me how to survive?"

Throughout our affair of eleven years,

disappearing into the pleasure-unto-death

acts I recall now as love and, afterward,

orbiting through the long, deep sleeps

in which memory, motor of everything,

reconstituted itself, I cared nothing about

life outside the walls of our bedroom.

The hand erasing writes the real thing,

and I am trying. I loved life and see now

this was a weakness. I loved the little

births and deaths occurring in us daily.

Even the white spit on your sharp teeth

was the foam of love, saying to me: It is not true,

after all, that you were never loved.

EMBERS

Poor summer, it doesn't know it's dying.

A few days are all it has. Still, the lake

is with me, its strokes of blue-violet

and the fiery sun replacing loneliness.

I feel like an animal that has found a place.

This is my burrow, my nest, my attempt

to say, *I exist.* A rose can't shut itself

and be a bud again. It's a malady,

wanting it. On the shore, the moon sprinkles

light over everything, like a campfire,

and in the green-black night, the tall pines

hold their arms out as God held His arms

out to say that He was lonely and that

He was making Himself a man.

As I lie on my belly at the edge of the dock,

I hear sighing, plainly human, from behind a membrane.

Daylight leaks yellow and black, then everything goes raw.

I'm a boy again, setting the jib but messing it up;

the sigh—thin, acidic, austere—is my father's;

then I hear others: the sighs of wet trees bending

with apples, of gnats on the lake, and of young furrows

at the corners of my eyes; the sighs of duckweed

and pampas grass, of my sweat-moistened shirt

drawing bees like a flower, and of the nine Hells

under me biting the spirit because reason is triumphing

over the senses—all blame forgotten—as I sprawl

on warm wooden boards in the shadow of autumn leaves,

watching you crawl through clear water toward me.

III

DUNE

BEACH WALK

I found a baby shark on the beach.

Seagulls had eaten his eyes. His throat was bleeding.

Lying on shell and sand, he looked smaller than he was.

The ocean had scraped his insides clean.

When I poked his stomach, darkness rose up in him,

like black water. Later, I saw a boy,

aroused and elated, beckoning from a dune.

Like me, he was alone. Something tumbled between us—

not quite emotion. I could see the pink

interior flesh of his eyes. "I got lost. Where am I?"

he asked, like a debt owed to death.

I was pressing my face to its spear-hafts.

We fall, we fell, we are falling. Nothing mitigates it.

The dark embryo bares its teeth and we move on.

Eating the peach, I feel like a murderer.

Time and darkness mean nothing to me,

moving forward and back with my white enameled teeth

and bloated tongue sating themselves on moist,

pulpy flesh. When I suck at the pit that resembles

a small mammal's skull, it erases all memory

of trouble and strife, of loneliness and the blindings

of erotic love, and of the blueprint of a world

in which man, hater of reason, cannot make

things right again. Eating the peach, I feel the long

wandering, my human hand—once fin and paw—

reaching through and across the allegory of Eden,

mud, boredom, and disease, to bees, solitude,

and a thousand hairs of grass blowing by chill waters.

DEAD WREN

When I open your little gothic wings

on my whitewashed chest of drawers,

I almost fear you, as if today were my funeral.

Moment by moment, enzymes digest

your life into a kind of coffin liqueur.

Two flies, like coroners, investigate your feathers.

My clock is your obelisk, though only this morning

you lunged into my room, extravagant as Nero,

then, not seeing yourself in the sunlit glass,

struck it. Night—what beams does it clear away?

The rain falls. The sky is pained. All that breathes suffers.

Yet the waters of affliction are purifying.

The wounded soldier heals. There is new wine and oil.

Here, take my handkerchief as your hearse.

Hip-deep in the pit, wading through ruins

of that border state where the mind narrows

and will not be broadened by hope,

I hear your strong victorious voice

and almost believe love of country

will be enough to right old wrongs,

pity the poor, and avert war,

but then the soft-pedaling language resumes,

you lick your lips nervously,

veering toward arrogance,

and my head aches all over again.

What I see are tactical endurance,

rhetoric divorced from practice, and aversion

squatting on a shaky platform.

When you place your hand on the Bible,

do you think about eternal questions:

Why are we here instead of nothing?

Does love make us who we are?

Do we survive death? Like Jesus,

my father's people were sprinkled on their foreheads;

they farmed peaches and tobacco.

My mother's people fled invading armies

of Romans, Persians, and Turks.

Can a few like you lead us all?

Waving from your droning black helicopter

at the cheering hordes, fixing your gaze

on some mythical past, can you see

time battering the surface of Earth?

Can you see sorrow is egalitarian?

Or the hairy leg of Satan planted firmly

in poverty, where the birth of suffering

supersedes the birth of perfect children?

Nature seems complacent

as hate rains down on us in swoops.

Why does God make man feel it?

Part of me, the real red-bloodedness,

open, drinking in the night, hates something vaguely, too,

and is frightened, staring out at the night grass

where, when the moon breaks out for a minute,

steam rises from ropes of excrement

extruded by some unbroken animal

circling in the dark wood.

HYMN

After a stormy night, with thunder peals,

I went out for coffee and found a woman

in a wheelbarrow, speaking in a low voice

to no one in particular, the *is* of her life

wholly stripped away, her once pretty face

hardened into a triangle, and I thought:

"What one wants, to be a person who fully loves,

seems so focused and pure." The sun hadn't risen.

Living things flew around. The city crept up,

like a green blade out of a chasm emitting

plumes of vapor. All the people of the world

seemed to look away as water drops fell on us

from air conditioners and a terrible instrument

struck down out of a depthless blue sky.

(Firing weapons in a prolonged fusillade,
attacking militants left fifty-eight dead.)

In the hills, a boy drove a donkey cart;

women carried bundles of sticks on their heads;

a dog's bark echoed off the ivory rock;

a lost bee, blood-sticky little almsman,

bathed in a water trough. If every man has a soul,

these had fled or were fermenting.

Free at least from all pain,

the stunted figures lay like rag dolls.

Broken eyeglasses, a tangled earring,

tawny footprints leading nowhere deep,

deep inside the birth colonnade:

The lowing heifer tugged to the altar two thousand

years ago now wore a sad human face.

Why must God always side with the brave?

PERSIMMON TREE

From my bare patch of earth,

I feel the night air against my skin.

Tomorrow, when the weather is dry,

a weary farmer will unfold his scrubbed body

onto the fertile soil under me.

I like to glance down at him

napping on my yellow leaves.

In summer, I see him mowing the field,

in winter, walking alone across the lake ice.

He seems different from the others;

and sometimes, wandering the forest,

where elder and lilac obscure the path

and no one goes but goats,

he forgets the predatory, domineering impulse.

See, I say to myself, he was supposed to be enslaved,

but he's not. Over and over,

I wonder about him.

Once, I lived through a bombing

and watched the wild and ghastly light

go out of a soldier's face.

His skin was white as snow on the mountains.

Death is nothing compared to the pain

that comes before.

At times, my life seems merely a root left behind for others

sampling my fruit, scooping the flesh out.

The air around me loses its moisture

and the sun is laid waste by darkness,

forty times dark,

but this, I've found, is only a trick —

peremptory, savage—

because light always reemerges

and once again illuminates—

like a white moth naked on a leaf—

the deep ravine where I live,

eighty-seven years now,

thirty-three feet tall,

with male and female flowers,

sick, I confess, of the human pendulum's

drift between the chaos of revenge

and the smooth order of forgiveness.

Poor Man, kind and apprehensive,

he looks at himself but cannot see

the beauty of his free will unless

he's suffering at the hands of it.

BEES

Poured through the bees, the sunlight, like flesh

and spirit, emits a brightness pushing everything

else away except the bees' vibrating bronze bodies

riding the air as if on strings that flex

and kick back as they circle the hive outside

my window, where they are cheerful and careful

in their work, their audible bee-voices

in solidarity with summer, as it is getting on,

and all the leaves of the forest quiver toward

nothingness on Earth, where we are all fallen

and where we sin and betray in order

to love and where the germinating seeds

of the soul are watered by tears of loneliness,

fear, and emotional revenge.

MIRROR

After a season of war, darkness retreated

into darkness, and I thought: Now things will be different.

Hunting for mushrooms at the lake, I found youthful

men and women sunning themselves, while rabbits

hopped about. Darkness had made everything brighter.

At home, I sautéed porcini in butter, with garlic and parsley.

The chaos of life synthesized into something beautiful.

Seepages of violence receded. Even the blackbirds,

squealing in long-haired willows, fused in my mind with love,

instead of giving sorrow sound. Then in the mirror,

my body shone silvery white, like an ember

(what was my life?), but it was only the naked,

simpler me remembering the old pain of seeing.

Like a juicy worm in straw, it wanted to be fed.

I have a fever which I'm treating with gin.

A war is lingering, but I feel distanced from it.

I think I'm at the lowest level of actual control,

lying around in black swimming trunks,

staring out at treetops and cobalt blue,

an innocent combination pouring hunger

through my heart. A pink butterfly capers

over the cosmos, where it got lost this morning.

Is it straight from God, the freedom?

I want to write something highly controlled

that is the opposite, like a dizzy

honeycomb gleaming with amber light.

I love the light of the water shellacking

my arms and legs, like something from Ovid.

Each day begins with lavender light

moving through my room, like an open hand,

and the call of birds out my window

and butter-and-eggs and adult bees searching

for the sweet, white, four-petaled violets

and hunchbacked loons in flight, projecting

their feet out behind, like me in my twin bed,

pressing my face into nothing, until afternoon

arrives, and I swim across the bay under

a white sun, its arms beckoning over

endless blue, my back and shoulders darkening,

like the raked earth. I feel protection

under the law, if the law is light. In the woods,

afterward, I pick blueberries.

While I am writing this, the cat scratches herself

and rubs her belly against my knees, purring.

She'll stretch out soon on my books and bills.

On the horizon, a sailboat is going nowhere:

Remain a while, drink a cocktail, it pleads,

and I do. How sad my footprints look

in the dunes, like a single voice

raised in lament, looking for liberation.

A white cloud overhead moves too quickly,

casting shadows, and all the people of the shore say,

"Oh, how lovely," but I don't believe it is at all.

I think of something being extinguished.

Sometimes, I feel like a large, open eye,

in which there is a sifting of too many things:

a summer fever, brushstrokes of green larches,

yellow rayflowers, Japanese beetles copulating

everywhere, war, and a cut-glass tumbler of gin—

all these scraps, like some eternal revenue

of memory and feeling blown together.

My lips nibble out of control,

like creatures differentiating themselves,

trying to give inwardness voice. "Oh,

let him be," God is saying, "I made him."

Down on the lawn, a campfire snaps violently

as the coals are stirred with a poker,

burning the beetles in frenzied masses.

Still, the earth forms, stems flourish,

and the time of my life goes on.

Yesterday, a storm tore the bay apart.

I was swimming and became disoriented.

Violent scrolls of foam and green water

rolled across the silky, pellucid surface

and lightning stained everything red

as I stroked through showers of arrows.

The little tree of knowledge with my name on it

wasn't anywhere for me to climb onto.

Throw a man into the sea and he becomes a fish,

but still, the sound was unsettling—

its foaming energy, its vibrant mutability.

Then I lay face down in wet sand,

my arms strung with strands of seaweed,

as I rolled over, trembling,

and a solid blackbird flew into view,

catching a bee in its mouth, calling to mind

the purple wild thyme that grows on lawns

in these Northern parts, tawny bees murmuring

over them on their way home to sleep and safety,

remaking them when nature beats them apart,

putting their whole lives into the small sting

that hurts us, but not before changing gum

into gold, like poetry, which is stronger

than I am and makes me do what it wants.

Is there something in earth that makes us resemble them—

rising at dawn, the sun flashing scarlet,

rubbing together for warmth, going forward—

even when the world seems just a heap of broken things?

ACKNOWLEDGMENTS

For their encouragement, I am indebted to the editors of the following publications, where poems, sometimes in different form, were originally published.

The American Poetry Review: "The Lost Bee," "Mirror," "Self-portrait with Hornets." *The Atlantic Monthly*: "Birthday" and "Dead Wren." *The New Republic*: "Embers." *The New Yorker*: "American Kestrel," "Bowl of Lilacs," "Gravity and Center," "Gulls," "Homosexuality," "Poppies," "Self-portrait with Red Eyes," "To the Forty-third President," "The Tree Cutters," and "Twilight." *The Paris Review*: "Haircut" and "Sycamores." *Ploughshares*: "To Sleep." *Poetry Northwest*: "Ambulance." *Salmagundi*: "Beach Walk" and "Toxicology." *Slate*: "Eating the Peach." *The Threepenny Review*: "The Erasers" and "Oil & Steel." *The Yale Review*: "Loons" and "Shaving."

I would also like to record my thanks to the John Simon Guggenheim Memorial Foundation for a grant that was of great help in writing this book. My thanks also to the Blue Mountain Center, Hawthornden Castle, the Liguria Study Center, and the Bellagio Study and Conference Center for their hospitality and for solitude during residencies.

Printed in the USA
CPSIA information can be obtained
at www.ICGtesting.com
LVHW091148150724
785511LV00005B/628

9 780374 531126